W9-BAH-884

Centipedes and Millipedes Are Gross!

Leigh Rockwood

PowerKiDS press

New York

Published in 2011 by The Rosen Publishing Group, Inc.
29 East 21st Street, New York, NY 10010

First Edition

Editor: Maggie Murphy
Book Design: Ashley Burrell
Photo Researcher: Kate Laczynski

Photo Credits: Cover, pp. 4, 5, 8, 9, 10, 11, 13 (bottom left), 18, 21, 22 Shutterstock.com; p. 6 © www.iStockphoto.com/jeridu; p. 7 Jason Edwards/Getty Images; p. 12 © Hecker/Sauer/age fotostock; p. 13 (top) © www.iStockphoto.com/Michael Pettigrew; p. 13 (bottom right) George Grall/Getty Images; p. 14–15 © www.iStockphoto.com/Jeffrey Hochstrasser; p. 16 © Bartomeu Borrell/age fotostock; p. 17 © www.iStockphoto.com/Cathy Keifer; p. 19 © www.iStockphoto.com/Vladimir Davydov; p. 20 © www.iStockphoto.com/Ralton Bentley.

Library of Congress Cataloging-in-Publication Data

Rockwood, Leigh.
  Centipedes and millipedes are gross! / Leigh Rockwood. — 1st ed.
    p. cm. — (Creepy crawlies)
  Includes index.
  ISBN 978-1-4488-0701-7 (library binding) — ISBN 978-1-4488-1363-6 (pbk.) — ISBN 978-1-4488-1364-3 (6-pack)
  1. Centipedes—Juvenile literature. 2. Millipedes—Juvenile literature. I. Title.
  QL449.5.C53 2011
  595.6'2—dc22
                                   2010007717

Manufactured in the United States of America

CPSIA Compliance Information: Batch #WS10PK: For Further Information contact Rosen Publishing, New York, New York at 1-800-237-9932

Contents

Leggy Bugs!

Have you ever been surprised to see a bug that has what seems like too many legs to count? That bug was likely either a centipede or millipede. These small animals both look like weird worms with many legs. However, as **arthropods**, they are

This is a millipede. Millipedes generally have many more legs than centipedes do.

This is a centipede. Most centipedes have flatter bodies than millipedes do.

related more closely to insects and crustaceans than worms. Both centipedes and millipedes also live on or under the ground.

When you see centipedes or millipedes, they are likely looking for food. Millipedes eat mostly rotting plants and centipedes eat other bugs. That seems pretty gross, but this makes these creepy crawlies helpful to people.

At first, you might think centipedes and millipedes look a lot alike. However, these gross animals are not very closely related to each other. Most centipedes have flat bodies. Their bodies are **segmented**. Each of their 15 to 177 body segments has one pair of legs on it. The body segment behind the head has a pair of sharp claws called forcipules.

Both centipedes and millipedes have antennae. Here you can see this centipede's long antennae, at the top of its head.

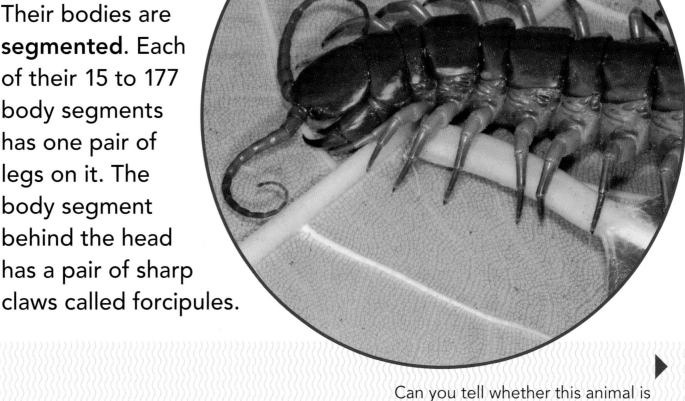

Can you tell whether this animal is a centipede or a millipede? It is a millipede! You can tell because it has two pairs of legs on each segment.

Centipedes use forcipules to catch and poison their **prey**.

Millipedes' bodies tend to look rounder than those of centipedes. They have two pairs of legs on each of their 25 to 100 body segments. Although they have twice as many legs, millipedes move much slower than centipedes do. Their many legs help them dig in the soil.

Different Lives

Although centipedes and millipedes look a bit like each other, they lead very different lives. They are so different that scientists put them in two different groupings called classes. Centipedes belong to a class of arthropods called Chilopoda. Millipedes belong to a class called Diplopoda.

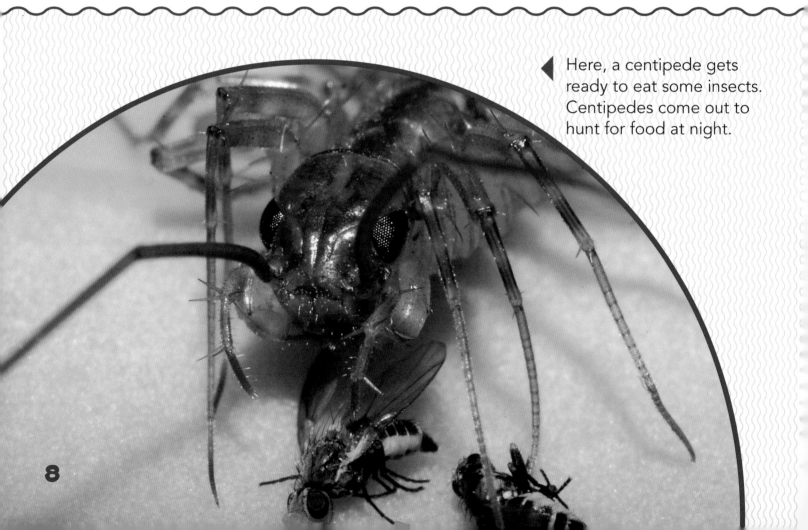

Here, a centipede gets ready to eat some insects. Centipedes come out to hunt for food at night.

Millipedes are slow movers. Their many legs move in a wavelike way when they crawl.

One of the biggest differences between centipedes and millipedes is what they eat. Centipedes are **predators**. When they hunt for food, they move quickly. They use their forcipules to kill their prey, which is mostly spiders and bugs. Millipedes are **decomposers**. They move slowly and eat dead leaves and other rotting plant matter. Predators and decomposers are different yet important parts of **food chains**.

9

Where do these many-legged creepy crawlies live? Both centipedes and millipedes live throughout the world. Both animals like wet, dark places that are not too cold.

Millipedes live among the rotting plant matter they eat. They also tunnel into leaves and under the soil to hide or rest. Centipedes often stay

Here, a centipede crawls across tree bark.

This millipede is climbing a leafy plant.

under rocks, bark, and other plant matter when they are not hunting for food. You may have seen a gross, squiggly house centipede in your house. It likely lives in dark corners of the cellar or closet and comes out only at night.

Life Cycle

1

Centipedes and millipedes have parts of their life cycles in common. Most centipedes and millipedes hatch from eggs as **larvae**. These larvae look like adult centipedes and millipedes, but they are smaller and have fewer segments.

2

As the larvae grow, they **molt**. Each molting adds another leg-bearing segment. These molting and growing periods are called instars. Most centipedes and millipedes go through about six or seven instars before they reach adulthood.

Most centipedes and millipedes live for about a year or two. Sometimes, though, they can live as long as six years. However, most are not lucky enough to live that long!

Adult male and female centipedes and millipedes **mate** to make babies. Then, females lay eggs in the dirt. Sometimes, the female will cover them with sticky matter her body makes, to help keep the eggs safe from predators.

3

Fact Sheet: Gross!

1 Tiny animals called mites live on the giant African millipede's exoskeleton. These mites do not hurt the millipede. They help keep the exoskeleton clean!

2 Some millipedes that live in dark caves glow in the dark!

3 Centipedes and millipedes have poor eyesight. Some do not even have eyes. Scientists believe these animals communicate using the senses of touch and smell.

4 Garden millipedes may live in a greenhouse and hurt the plants there. They may also come into your home during the cooler months of the year!

Scientists think that centipedes and millipedes were one of the first kinds of animals to live on land, millions of years ago. Before then, all animals had lived in water.

5

The largest millipede in the world was a giant African millipede owned by Jim Klinger of Coppell, Texas. It was 15.2 inches (38.6 cm) long!

6

There are about 3,000 different species of centipedes and about 10,000 species of millipedes.

7

"Centipede" and "millipede" are names that come from Latin. "Centipede" means "hundred-footed" and "millipede" means "thousand-footed."

8

Centipedes on the Hunt

Centipedes hunt at night. They move quickly and use the poison in the glands near their forcipules to kill their prey. Most centipedes eat earthworms, bugs, and spiders. Some tropical species are as long as 11 inches (28 cm) and are big enough to kill small birds or lizards!

This hungry centipede is eating its prey. Meat-eating animals, such as centipedes, are called carnivores.

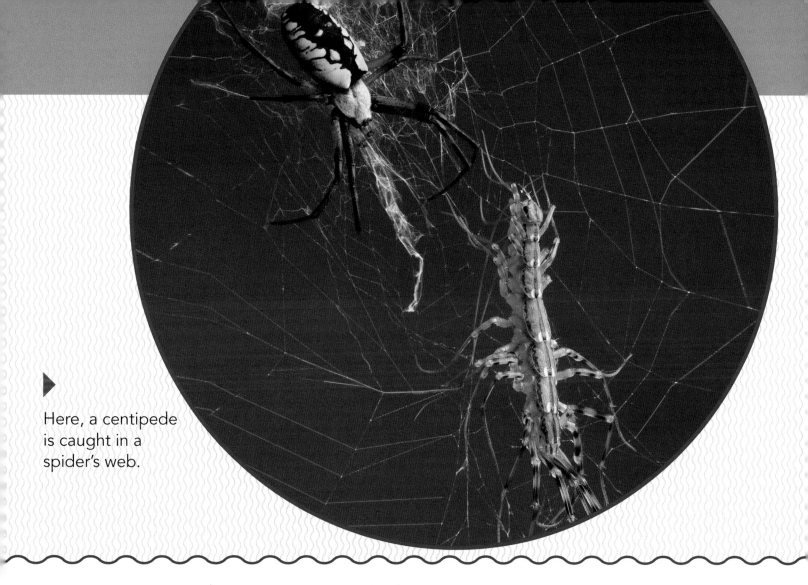

Here, a centipede is caught in a spider's web.

Centipedes are prey for many animals. Birds, spiders, small snakes, toads, and lizards all eat centipedes. Centipedes will try to run away from or hide from predators. If that does not work, they will bite. Centipedes sometimes bite people. Although the bite may hurt or swell, it is generally not a deadly bite.

Millipedes eat rotting plant matter. Some species even eat animal waste! Millipedes have special organisms in their guts that help them break these things down into the **nutrients** they need. Many schools keep pet millipedes in classrooms because they are easy to care for and do not hurt people.

This flat-looking millipede is sometimes called a tractor millipede. It feeds on rotting plants in Southeast Asian rain forests.

This is what a millipede looks like when it curls up into a spiral.

Many of the same predators that eat centipedes also eat millipedes. Millipedes are not fast on their many feet. Instead of running from predators, they roll up into a ball or spiral. Their hard exoskeletons help keep them safe. Some millipedes also let out a bad-smelling, bad-tasting, or poisonous liquid or gas.

The Giant African Millipede

The giant African millipede is one of the world's largest species of millipede. It lives in the **rain forests** of western Africa. Adults are around 8 to 11 inches (20–28 cm) long. That is more than four times the size of the millipedes you might see in a North American backyard!

Giant African millipedes are sometimes known as shongololos in South Africa.

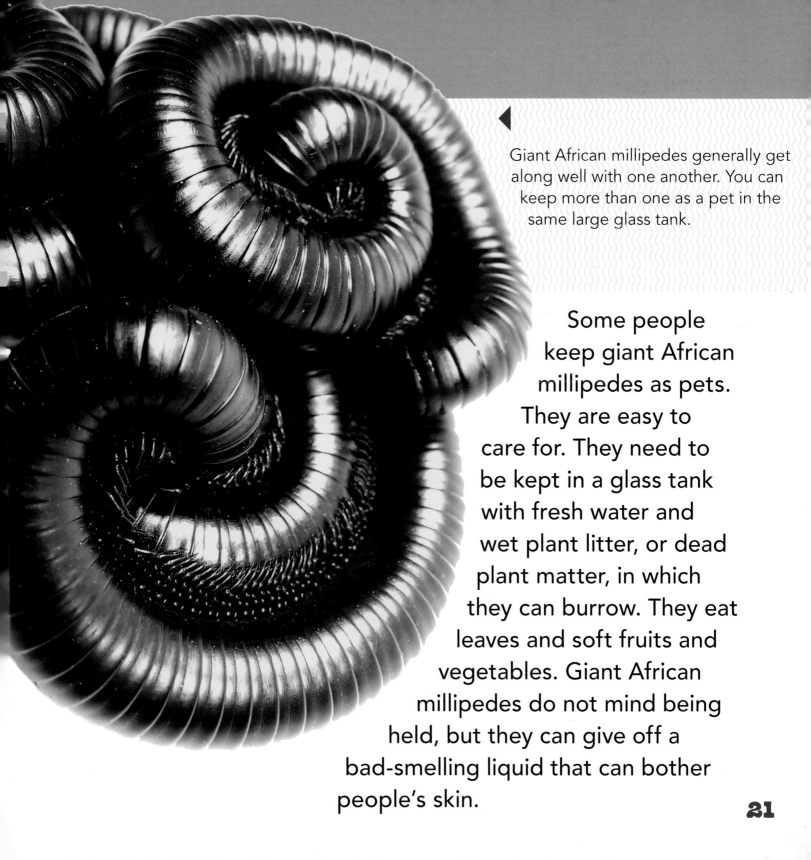

Giant African millipedes generally get along well with one another. You can keep more than one as a pet in the same large glass tank.

Some people keep giant African millipedes as pets. They are easy to care for. They need to be kept in a glass tank with fresh water and wet plant litter, or dead plant matter, in which they can burrow. They eat leaves and soft fruits and vegetables. Giant African millipedes do not mind being held, but they can give off a bad-smelling liquid that can bother people's skin.

Food chains link all the animals in a habitat to each other. Centipedes and millipedes are near the bottom of the food chain because many other animals eat them. When millipedes eat rotting plants, their waste adds nutrients to the soil so that new plants can grow, too!

Creepy crawlies, such as gross centipedes and millipedes, are important parts of the food chain!

Animals at the bottom of the food chain, such as centipedes and millipedes, help life on Earth keep going. Now you know that although centipedes and millipedes may be gross, they are part of your life!

Glossary

arthropods (AR-thruh-podz) The scientific name for a group of animals with jointed legs and hard outer coverings.

decomposers (dee-kum-POH-zerz) Living things that break down the cells of dead plants and animals into simpler parts.

exoskeleton (ek-soh-SKEH-leh-tun) The hard covering on the outside of an animal's body that holds and guards the soft insides.

food chains (FOOD CHAYNZ) Groups of living things that are each other's food.

larvae (LAHR-vee) Animals in the early period of life in which they have a wormlike form.

mate (MAYT) To join together to make babies.

molt (MOHLT) To shed hair, feathers, shell, horns, or skin.

nutrients (NOO-tree-unts) Food that a living thing needs to live and grow.

predators (PREH-duh-terz) Animals that kill other animals for food.

prey (PRAY) An animal that is hunted by another animal for food.

rain forests (RAYN FOR-ests) Thick forests that receive large amounts of rain during the year.

segmented (SEG-men-ted) Having many smaller pieces.

species (SPEE-sheez) Kinds of living things. All people are one species.

Index

A
arthropods, 4, 8

B
bodies, 6–7, 13

C
claws, 6
crustaceans, 5

D
decomposers, 9

E
exoskeleton(s), 14, 19

F
food, 5, 9, 11
food chain(s), 9, 22
forcipules, 6–7, 9, 16

L
larvae, 12
legs, 4, 6–7

N
nutrients, 18, 22

P
people, 5, 17–18, 21

plants, 5, 14, 22
predators, 9, 13, 17, 19
prey, 7, 9, 16–17

R
rain forests, 20

S
segment(s), 6–7, 12
soil, 7, 10, 22
species, 15–16, 18, 20

W
worms, 4–5, 16

Web Sites

Due to the changing nature of Internet links, PowerKids Press has developed an online list of Web sites related to the subject of this book. This site is updated regularly. Please use this link to access the list:
www.powerkidslinks.com/creep/centi/